MY JOURNEY TOWARDS FINANCIAL SUCCESS @ 35

SAHIL A GOSALIA

Learn
from the
BEST
MY JOURNEY
TOWARDS FINANCIAL
SUCCESS
@ 35
Sahil A Gosalia

Disclaimer: The information provided in this book, "My Journey Towards Financial Success at 35," is for educational and informational purposes only. It is not intended as financial or investment advice. The readers are advised to consult with a qualified financial professional or seek independent financial advice before making any financial decisions or implementing any strategies mentioned in this book. The author and publisher of this book are not responsible for any financial losses or damages incurred by the readers as a result of applying the information provided in this book.

The readers are solely responsible for their own financial decisions and actions. The examples and calculations provided in this book are for illustrative purposes only and may not accurately reflect actual financial situations or market conditions. Please note that laws and regulations related to personal finance and investing may vary by country or region, and it is important to be aware of and comply with the applicable laws and regulations in your specific jurisdiction.

Dedication

This book is dedicated to all young adults determined to control their financial future and achieve their dreams.

To those who are tired of living paycheck to paycheck and struggling to make ends meet, this book is for you. May it provide you with the knowledge, inspiration, and motivation you need to achieve financial success and live the life of your dreams.

To my family and friends, who have supported me on my own journey toward financial success, thank you for your love, encouragement, and guidance.

And finally, to my readers, I dedicate this book to you. May it empower you to take action, make positive changes in your financial life, and achieve the financial success and freedom you deserve.

Introduction

Are you tired of living paycheck to paycheck? Do you dream of retiring early and living the life of your dreams? Are you ready to take control of your financial future and achieve financial success at a young age?

If you answered "**yes**" to any of these questions, then this book is for you. "My Journey Towards Financial Success at 35: A Comprehensive Guide to Achieving Your Goals" is a step-by-step guide to help you achieve financial success and retire at age 35.

In this book, we will explore the key principles and strategies that are essential for achieving financial success, including establishing clear financial goals, building a strong financial foundation, maximizing your income, managing your expenses, investing for the future, building passive income streams, planning for retirement, managing risk, balancing money and life, and staying motivated and on track.

Through personal anecdotes, practical tips, and interactive exercises, we will guide you on your journey toward financial success. Whether you're just starting out or you're looking to take your finances to the next level, this book will provide you with the tools and strategies you need to achieve your financial goals and enjoy the freedom and security that comes with financial success.

So, are you ready to take control of your financial future and start your journey toward financial success at 35? **Let's begin!**

Table of Contents

Achieving financial success is a goal that many people aspire to, and with good reason. Being financially successful can mean having the freedom to pursue your passions, the security to weather unexpected financial challenges, and the ability to provide for yourself and your loved ones. In this book, we will explore the steps you can take to achieve financial success from a young age, starting at 21, and how you can retire at the age of 35.

Establishing Financial Goals

Before you can begin working towards financial success, you need to establish clear goals. In this chapter, we will discuss how to set financial goals that are achievable and realistic.

- Understanding your values and priorities
- Defining short-term and long-term financial goals
- Making a plan to achieve your goals
- Tracking your progress and making adjustments as needed

Building a Strong Financial Foundation

To achieve financial success, you need a strong foundation. In this chapter, we will explore the key elements of a strong financial foundation, including:

- Creating a budget and sticking to it
- Building an emergency fund
- Paying off high-interest debt
- Establishing credit

Maximizing Your Income

Increasing your income is an important part of achieving financial success. In this chapter, we will discuss strategies for maximizing your income, including:

- Pursuing education and training to increase your earning potential
- Starting a side hustle

- Negotiating a higher salary or promotion
- Investing in the stock market

Managing Your Expenses

While increasing your income is important, managing your expenses is equally important. In this chapter, we will explore strategies for managing your expenses, including:

- Minimizing your fixed expenses
- Cutting back on discretionary spending
- Shopping for bargains and deals
- Living frugally

Investing for the Future

Investing is a key component of achieving financial success. In this chapter, we will discuss the different types of investments and how to create an investment plan that works for you, including:

- Investing in stocks and bonds
- Creating a diversified portfolio
- Understanding risk and return
- Seeking the advice of a financial advisor

Building Passive Income Streams

Passive income streams can help you achieve financial success by providing a steady stream of income without requiring ongoing effort. In this chapter, we will explore different types of passive income streams, including:

- Real estate investing
- Dividend-paying stocks
- Peer-to-peer lending
- Creating and selling digital products

Planning for Retirement

Retiring at the age of 35 requires careful planning and

preparation. In this chapter, we will discuss strategies for planning for retirement, including:

- Determining your retirement goals and needs
- Calculating how much you need to save
- Creating a retirement plan
- Maximizing tax-advantaged retirement accounts

Managing Risk

Managing risk is an important part of achieving financial success. In this chapter, we will discuss different types of risk and how to manage them, including:

- Investment risk
- Job loss risk
- Health and disability risk
- Liability risk

Balancing Money and Life

Achieving financial success is not just about accumulating wealth; it's also about finding a balance between money and life. In this chapter, we will explore strategies for finding this balance, including:

- Pursuing your passions and interests
- Traveling and experiencing new things

- Giving back to your community
- Creating a fulfilling personal life

Staying Motivated and On Track

Achieving financial success requires discipline, hard work, and dedication. In this chapter, we will discuss strategies for staying motivated and on track, including:

- Surrounding yourself with supportive people
- Celebrating small successes along the way
- Holding yourself accountable
- Continuing to learn and grow

It is possible to achieve financial success from a young age, but it requires dedication, hard work, and a willingness to learn and grow. By following the strategies outlined in this book, you can establish clear financial goals, build a strong foundation, maximize your income, manage your expenses, invest for the future, plan for retirement, manage risk, balance money and life, and stay motivated and on track. With these tools, you can achieve financial success and retire at the age of 35.

CHAPTER

Establishing Financial Goals

Establishing financial goals is the first step towards achieving financial success. Without clear goals, it's difficult to know where you're headed, and it's even harder to create a plan to get there. In this chapter, we will discuss how to set financial goals that are achievable and realistic.

Understanding your values and priorities

Before you can set financial goals, it's important to understand your values and priorities. Your values are the most important things in life, such as family, health, education, and career. You need to focus on your priorities to achieve your values, such as saving money, investing in your education, or starting a business.

Take some time to reflect on your values and priorities. What matters most to you? What are your long-term goals? What are your short-term goals? What are the things that you need to focus on right now to achieve your long-term goals?

Defining short-term and long-term financial goals

Once you clearly understand your values and priorities, it's time to define your financial goals. Financial goals can be categorized into short-term and long-term goals.

You can achieve short-term goals within the next year or two. Examples of short-term financial goals might include:

- Creating an emergency fund

- Paying off credit card debt
- Saving for a down payment on a home
- Investing in a retirement account

Long-term goals are goals you can achieve over a longer period, typically five years or more. Examples of long-term financial goals might include:

- Paying off student loan debt
- Saving for a Child's college education
- Buying a second home or investment property
- Retiring by a certain age

When setting financial goals, it's important to be specific and measurable. Instead of saying, "**I want to save more money,**" try setting a specific goal, such as "**I want to save $10,000 for a down payment on a home by the end of the year.**"

Making a plan to achieve your goals

Once you have defined your financial goals, it's time to create a plan to achieve them. This plan should include specific steps that you will take to reach your goals, as well as a timeline for when you expect to achieve them.

Start by breaking your goals down into smaller, more manageable tasks. For example, if your goal is to pay off credit card debt, break it down into smaller tasks such as:

- Stop using credit cards for non-essential purchases
- Create a budget and stick to it
- Make larger than minimum payments on your credit card debt each month
- Negotiate a lower interest rate with your credit card company

Once you have broken your goals down into smaller tasks, create a timeline for when you expect to achieve each one. Be realistic about your timeline, and be willing to adjust it as needed. It's better to set a realistic timeline and achieve your goals than to set an unrealistic timeline and become discouraged when you don't meet it.

Tracking your progress and making adjustments as needed

Finally, it's important to track your progress towards your financial goals and make adjustments as needed. This will help you stay motivated and make sure that you are on track to achieve your goals.

There are several ways to track your progress towards your financial goals. You might create a spreadsheet to track your income, expenses, and savings. You might use a budgeting app to help you stay on track with your spending. You might even create a vision board or other visual representation of your goals to help keep you motivated.

As you track your progress, be willing to make adjustments as needed. If you find that you are not making as much progress as you had hoped, adjust your plan and timeline accordingly. If you are making more progress than expected, consider setting new, more challenging goals to push yourself further.

Staying motivated and committed

Setting financial goals is just the first step towards achieving financial success. To truly succeed, you must stay motivated and committed to your goals, even when things get tough. Here are a few strategies for staying motivated and committed to your financial goals:

- **Celebrate small successes along the way:** Celebrating small successes can help keep you motivated and remind you of why you set your goals in the first place. Whether it's paying off a credit card or saving a certain amount of money, take time to celebrate your accomplishments.

- **Surround yourself with supportive people:** Surrounding yourself with supportive people who share your values and goals can help keep you motivated and on track. Find a mentor or join a support group to help you stay focused on your goals.

- **Hold yourself accountable:** Holding yourself accountable for your progress can help keep you motivated and focused on your goals. Keep track of your progress, set deadlines for yourself, and hold yourself accountable for meeting them.

- **Continue to learn and grow:** The more you learn about personal finance and investing, the more confident and motivated you will become. Take courses, read books and blogs, and attend seminars and workshops to continue to grow your knowledge and skills.

Conclusion

Establishing financial goals is the first step towards achieving financial success. By understanding your values and priorities, defining short-term and long-term financial goals, making a plan to achieve your goals, tracking your progress, and staying motivated and committed, you can achieve financial success and retire at the age of 35. Remember, achieving financial success takes time, effort, and dedication, but the rewards are well worth it.

CHAPTER

Building a Strong Financial Foundation

Building a strong financial foundation is critical to achieving long-term financial success. Establishing healthy financial habits early in life is important, starting with a strong financial foundation. This chapter will discuss the key components of building a strong financial foundation, including budgeting, saving, managing debt, and protecting your finances.

Budgeting

Budgeting is the foundation of good financial management. It allows you to plan your spending and ensure that you are living within your means. A budget is a financial plan that helps you allocate your income towards your expenses, savings, and investments. A budget will help you keep track of your money, identify areas where you can cut back on spending, and ensure that you are meeting your financial goals.

There are many budgeting strategies to choose from, but the most important thing is to find a strategy that works for you. **One popular strategy is the 50/30/20 rule. This rule suggests that you allocate 50% of your income towards needs (such as rent/mortgage, utilities, food), 30% towards wants (such as entertainment, dining out), and 20% towards savings and debt repayment.**

As motivational speaker Les Brown once said, "**Your goals are the roadmaps that guide you and show you what is possible for your life.**"

Saving

Saving is another critical component of building a strong financial foundation. Saving helps you achieve your financial goals, build an emergency fund, and prepare for unexpected expenses. Saving money is not always easy, but it is essential to achieving financial success.

One of the best ways to save money is to make it automatic. Set up automatic transfers from your checking account to a savings account each month. This will ensure that you are consistently saving money and making progress towards your financial goals.

Another way to save money is to find ways to reduce your expenses. Look for areas where you can cut back on spending, such as dining out or entertainment. Small changes can add up over time and make a big difference in your overall financial picture.

Managing Debt

Managing debt is another critical component of building a strong financial foundation. Debt can be a powerful tool when used correctly, but it can also be a source of stress and financial hardship when mismanaged.

One way to manage debt is to prioritize paying off high-interest debt first, such as credit card debt. High-interest debt can quickly spiral out of control and can be difficult to pay off if you are only making minimum payments.

Another strategy for managing debt is to consolidate debt into a single loan with a lower interest rate. This can make it easier to manage debt and can save you money in interest payments over time.

As financial guru Dave Ramsey once said, "**You must gain control over your money or the lack of it will forever control you.**"

Protecting Your Finances

Protecting your finances is another important component of building a strong financial foundation. Protecting your finances involves taking steps to prevent fraud, identity theft, and other financial crimes. It also involves protecting your assets and ensuring that you have adequate insurance coverage.

One way to protect your finances is to monitor your accounts regularly for fraudulent activity. Review your bank and credit card statements each month and report any suspicious activity immediately.

Another way to protect your finances is to use strong passwords and enable two-factor authentication on all of your accounts. This will make it more difficult for hackers to access your accounts and steal your personal information.

Conclusion

Building a strong financial foundation is critical to achieving long-term financial success. By establishing healthy financial habits early in life, including budgeting, saving, managing debt, and protecting your finances, you can achieve your financial goals and build a secure financial future. Remember, achieving financial success takes time, effort, and dedication, but the rewards are well worth

CHAPTER

Maximizing Your Income

Maximizing your income is a key component of achieving financial success. The more money you earn, the more you can save and invest, and the faster you can achieve your financial goals. In this chapter, we will discuss strategies for maximizing your income, including improving your earning potential, negotiating your salary, and pursuing additional income streams.

Improving Your Earning Potential

One of the best ways to maximize your income is to improve your earning potential. This involves developing your skills and education to become more valuable in the job market. The more valuable you are to employers, the more you can command in terms of salary and benefits.

There are many ways to improve your earning potential, including:

1. **Pursue additional education or training:** Investing in additional education or training can make you more valuable in the job market. Consider pursuing a degree or certification in your field, or taking courses to develop new skills.

2. **Seek out mentorship:** Find a mentor in your industry who can help you develop your skills and

provide guidance on career advancement.

3. **Network:** Building a strong professional network can help you learn about new job opportunities and connect with people who can help you advance in your career.

4. **Stay up-to-date on industry trends:** Keeping up with trends and developments in your industry can make you more valuable to employers.

Brian Tracy once said, "**Investing in yourself is the best investment you will ever make. It will not only improve your life; it will improve the lives of all those around you.**"

Negotiating Your Salary

Negotiating your salary is another key component of maximizing your income. Many people are afraid to negotiate their salary, but it is important to remember that employers expect it. Negotiating your salary can make a significant difference in your earning potential over time.

Here are some tips for negotiating your salary:

1. Research salary ranges for your position: Before negotiating your salary, research what others in your position are earning. This will give you a baseline to work from and help you negotiate a fair salary.

2. Highlight your value: During the negotiation process, highlight the value that you bring to the

company. This can include your skills, experience, and education.

3. Be confident: Confidence is key when negotiating your salary. Practice what you are going to say ahead of time, and be assertive in your requests.

4. Be willing to compromise: Negotiating your salary is a give-and-take process. Be willing to compromise on certain aspects of your salary package in exchange for other benefits, such as additional vacation time or a flexible schedule.

As Tony Robbins once said, "**Identify your problems but give your power and energy to solutions.**"

Pursuing Additional Income Streams

In addition to improving your earning potential and negotiating your salary, pursuing additional income streams can also help maximize your income. Additional income streams can include part-time jobs, freelancing, or starting a side business.

Here are some ideas for pursuing additional income streams:

- Freelance: If you have a marketable skill, such as writing, graphic design, or programming, consider freelancing in your spare time.
- Rent out your space: If you have extra space in your home, consider renting it out on Airbnb or other short-term rental platforms.

- Sell items online: If you have items that you no longer need, consider selling them online through platforms such as eBay or Craigslist.
- Start a side business: If you have an entrepreneurial spirit, consider starting a side business in your spare time.

As entrepreneur and author Tim Ferriss once said, **"The goal is not to simply eliminate the bad, but to pursue and experience the best in the world."**

Invest in Stock Market

Investing in the stock market is another way to maximize your income and grow your wealth. It can be a powerful tool for achieving financial success, but it's important to approach it with caution and informed decision-making.

Before you start investing in the stock market, it's important to have a clear understanding of your financial goals, risk tolerance, and investment timeline. You should also educate yourself about the basics of investing in the stock market, including how it works, the different types of investments available, and the associated risks and potential rewards.

One important factor to consider when investing in the stock market is diversification. This means investing in a variety of different companies and industries to spread out your risk and minimize the impact of any single investment on your overall portfolio. As Warren Buffett, one of the most successful investors of all time, once said, "Diversification is a protection against ignorance. It makes little sense if you know what you are doing."

Another key factor to consider is your investment strategy. Some investors prefer to take a more active approach, researching and selecting individual stocks based on their analysis of the company and the market. Others prefer a more passive approach, investing in index funds or exchange-traded funds (ETFs) that track the performance of a particular market or sector.

Regardless of your investment strategy, it's important to stay informed and stay disciplined. This means regularly monitoring your investments, rebalancing your portfolio as needed, and avoiding emotional decision-making based on short-term market fluctuations.

As with any investment, there is always risk involved in investing in the stock market. It's important to remember that investing is a long-term game and that short-term volatility and fluctuations are to be expected. As legendary investor Peter Lynch once said, "In this business, if you're good, you're right six times out of ten. You're never going to be right nine times out of ten."

Conclusion

Maximizing your income is a key component of achieving financial success. By improving your earning potential, negotiating your salary, and pursuing additional income streams, you can increase your income and achieve your financial goals faster.

It is important to remember that maximizing your income is not just about the money. It is also about finding fulfillment and purpose in your career and life. As motivational speaker Jim Rohn once said, **"Happiness is not something you postpone for the future; it is something you design for the present."**

Take the time to invest in yourself, develop your skills, and pursue opportunities that align with your values and passions. By doing so, you can create a fulfilling and financially rewarding career.

Remember, financial success is a journey, not a destination. It requires commitment, hard work, and a willingness to take risks and pursue new opportunities. As entrepreneur and author Robert Kiyosaki once said, "**In the real world, the smartest people are people who make mistakes and learn. In school, the smartest people don't make mistakes.**"

So, take action, learn from your mistakes, and keep moving forward towards your financial goals. With dedication and persistence, you can maximize your income and achieve financial success.

CHAPTER

Managing Your Expenses

Managing your expenses is a critical component of achieving financial success. No matter how much you earn, if you don't manage your expenses effectively, you'll find it difficult to achieve your financial goals.

In this chapter, we'll explore some strategies for managing your expenses effectively, including setting a budget, tracking your spending, reducing unnecessary expenses, and developing a frugal mindset.

Setting a Budget

One of the most important steps in managing your expenses is setting a budget. A budget is a plan for your spending that helps you allocate your money effectively and avoid overspending. Without a budget, it's easy to spend more than you earn and accumulate debt.

To create a budget, start by tracking your income and expenses for a month. This will give you an idea of where your money is going and help you identify areas where you can reduce your spending. Once you have a clear understanding of your income and expenses, you can set a budget that allocates your money to different categories, such as housing, transportation, food, and entertainment.

When setting a budget, it's important to be realistic and flexible. Don't set a budget that's too restrictive or you won't be able to stick to it. Instead, set a budget that allows for some flexibility and adjustments as needed.

Tracking Your Spending

Another important strategy for managing your expenses is tracking your spending. This means keeping track of every penny you spend, whether it's a cup of coffee or a new pair of shoes. By tracking your spending, you can identify areas where you're overspending and make adjustments to your budget as needed.

There are many ways to track your spending, from using a spreadsheet or budgeting app to simply writing down your expenses in a notebook. The key is to find a method that works for you and stick to it.

Reducing Unnecessary Expenses

Reducing unnecessary expenses is another important strategy for managing your expenses. This means cutting back on expenses that don't add value to your life, such as eating out too often, buying clothes you don't need, or subscribing to services you don't use.

To reduce unnecessary expenses, start by identifying areas where you're overspending. For example, if you're eating out every day for lunch, consider bringing your lunch from home instead. If you're buying new clothes every month, consider buying second-hand or only buying what you truly need.

Developing a Frugal Mindset

Finally, developing a frugal mindset is a key component of managing your expenses effectively. This means developing habits and attitudes that prioritize saving money and avoiding unnecessary expenses.

There are many ways to develop a frugal mindset, from learning to cook your own meals to using coupons and shopping sales. The key is to find strategies that work for you and incorporate them into your daily life.

As financial expert Dave Ramsey once said, **"A budget is telling your money where to go instead of wondering where it went."** By setting a budget, tracking your spending, reducing unnecessary expenses, and developing a frugal mindset, you can manage your expenses effectively and achieve your financial goals.

Tips for Managing Your Expenses

Now that we've discussed the strategies for managing your expenses, let's take a look at some tips that can help you put these strategies into practice:

- Cut Back on Impulse Buys

One of the biggest culprits of overspending is impulse buying. To reduce your impulse buys, try sticking to a shopping list and avoiding stores or websites that tempt you to overspend.

- Use Cash Instead of Credit

Using cash instead of credit can help you avoid overspending and accumulating debt. Try withdrawing a set amount of cash for each category of your budget (e.g. groceries, entertainment) and using only that cash for those expenses.

- Plan for Irregular Expenses

Irregular expenses, such as car repairs or annual insurance payments, can throw off your budget if you're not prepared for them. Plan for these expenses by setting aside a small amount of money each month in a separate savings account.

- Look for Ways to Save on Fixed Expenses

Fixed expenses, such as rent or car payments, can be difficult to reduce. However, there are often ways to save on these expenses, such as negotiating a lower rent or refinancing your car loan.

- Find Free or Low-Cost Alternatives to Entertainment

Entertainment can be a major expense for many people. Look for free or low-cost alternatives, such as visiting a local park, attending free community events, or using library resources.

Motivational Quotes on Managing Expenses

Here are some motivational quotes that can help inspire you to manage your expenses effectively:

- "Every time you borrow money, you're robbing your future self." - Nathan W. Morris
- "Money is a tool, not a goal. It is a means to an end, not an end in itself." - Suze Orman
- "A penny saved is a penny earned." - Benjamin Franklin
- "It's not about how much money you make, it's about how much money you keep." - Robert Kiyosaki
- "The ability to discipline yourself to delay gratification in the short term in order to enjoy greater rewards in the long term is the indispensable prerequisite for success." - Brian Tracy

Conclusion

Managing your expenses is a critical component of achieving financial success. By setting a budget, tracking your spending, reducing unnecessary expenses, and developing a frugal mindset, you can manage your expenses effectively and achieve your financial goals. Remember, it's not about how much money you make, it's about how much money you keep.

CHAPTER

Investing for the Future

Investing for the future is a key component of achieving financial success. By investing your money wisely, you can build wealth, create a passive income stream, and achieve your long-term financial goals. In this chapter, we'll discuss the basics of investing, the different types of investments, and how to build a diversified investment portfolio.

Investing Basics

Investing is the act of putting your money into an asset with the expectation of generating a return. The return can come in the form of capital gains (an increase in the asset's value) or income (such as dividends or interest).

There are many different types of investments, each with its own unique characteristics, benefits, and risks. Some of the most common types of investments include:

1. **Stocks**: Stocks are ownership shares in a company. When you buy a stock, you become a shareholder and have a claim on the company's assets and earnings.
2. **Bonds**: Bonds are debt securities issued by companies or governments. When you buy a bond, you are essentially loaning your money to the issuer and receiving interest payments in return.
3. **Mutual Funds:** A mutual fund is a pool of money from many investors that is managed by a professional fund manager. The fund invests in a variety of assets,

such as stocks and bonds, and investors receive a share of the returns.

4. **Exchange-Traded Funds (ETFs):** ETFs are similar to mutual funds, but they trade like stocks on an exchange. ETFs can provide investors with exposure to a wide range of assets, such as stocks, bonds, and commodities.
5. **Real Estate:** Real estate can be a good investment for those who are looking for a tangible asset. Real estate can provide both rental income and capital appreciation over time.
6. **Commodities:** Commodities are physical goods that are traded on exchanges, such as gold or oil. Commodities can provide diversification benefits to an investment portfolio.

Building a Diversified Investment Portfolio

One of the key principles of investing is diversification. Diversification means spreading your money across different types of assets and investments to reduce your overall risk. A diversified investment portfolio can help protect your money from market volatility and economic downturns.

To build a diversified investment portfolio, you should consider the following:

1. Asset Allocation: Asset allocation is the process of dividing your investment portfolio among different types of assets, such as stocks, bonds, and real estate. Your asset allocation should be based on

your investment goals, risk tolerance, and time horizon.

2. Risk Management: Risk management is the process of identifying and managing the risks associated with your investments. Some risks to consider include market risk, inflation risk, and liquidity risk.
3. Investment Strategy: Your investment strategy should be based on your investment goals and risk tolerance. Some common investment strategies include value investing, growth investing, and income investing.
4. Monitoring and Rebalancing: It's important to regularly monitor your investment portfolio and make adjustments as needed. This may include rebalancing your portfolio to maintain your desired asset allocation.

Investing Quotes to Motivate You

Here are some investing quotes that can help motivate you to invest for your future:

"The stock market is a device for transferring money from the impatient to the patient." - **Warren Buffett**

"In the long run, it's not just how much money you make that will determine your future prosperity. It's how much of that money you put to work by saving it and investing it." - **Peter Lynch**

"The four most dangerous words in investing are: 'this time it's different.'" - **Sir John Templeton**

"The best investment you can make is in your own abilities. Anything you can do to develop your own abilities or business will be more productive." - **Warren Buffett**

"The key to successful investing is not predicting the future, but learning from the past and understanding the present." - **Howard Marks**

"Risk comes from not knowing what you're doing." - **Warren Buffett**

"Investing should be more like watching paint dry or watching grass grow. If you want excitement, take $800 and go to Las Vegas." - **Paul Samuelson**

Types of Investments

Let's take a closer look at the different types of investments and how they work.

1. Stocks

Stocks are ownership shares in a company. When you buy a stock, you become a shareholder and have a claim on the company's assets and earnings. The value of a stock can fluctuate based on a variety of factors, such as the company's financial performance, economic conditions, and market trends.

Some benefits of investing in stocks include:

- Potential for capital gains: If the value of the stock increases, you can sell it for a profit.

- Dividend income: Some stocks pay dividends, which are a portion of the company's earnings paid to shareholders.
- Diversification: Investing in stocks can provide diversification benefits to an investment portfolio.

Some risks of investing in stocks include:

- Market volatility: The value of a stock can fluctuates based on a variety of factors, making it a more volatile investment.
- Company-specific risk: The value of a stock can also be impacted by company-specific risks, such as poor financial performance or management changes.

2. Bonds

Bonds are debt securities issued by companies or governments. When you buy a bond, you are essentially loaning your money to the issuer and receiving interest payments in return. The value of a bond can fluctuate based on interest rates and the creditworthiness of the issuer.

Some benefits of investing in bonds include:

- Fixed income: Bonds can provide a steady stream of income through interest payments.
- Diversification: Investing in bonds can provide diversification benefits to an investment portfolio.
- Lower risk: Bonds are generally considered a lower-risk investment compared to stocks.

Some risks of investing in bonds include:

- Interest rate risk: The value of a bond can fluctuate based on changes in interest rates.
- Credit risk: There is a risk that the issuer may default on the bond, which could result in a loss of principal.

3. Mutual Funds

A mutual fund is a pool of money from many investors that is managed by a professional fund manager. The fund invests in a variety of assets, such as stocks and bonds, and investors receive a share of the returns.

Some benefits of investing in mutual funds include:

- Professional management: The fund is managed by a professional fund manager, who makes investment decisions on behalf of the investors.
- Diversification: Investing in mutual funds can provide diversification benefits to an investment portfolio.
- Access to a variety of assets: Mutual funds can provide access to a wide range of assets, such as stocks, bonds, and commodities.

Some risks of investing in mutual funds include:

- Fees: Mutual funds can have higher fees compared to other investments.

- Lack of control: Investors do not have control over the individual investments in the fund.

4. **Exchange-Traded Funds (ETFs)**

ETFs are similar to mutual funds, but they trade like stocks on an exchange. ETFs can provide investors with exposure to a wide range of assets, such as stocks, bonds, and commodities.

Some benefits of investing in ETFs include:

- Diversification: Investing in ETFs can provide diversification benefits to an investment portfolio.
- Lower fees: ETFs tend to have lower fees compared to mutual funds.

- Trading flexibility: ETFs can be bought and sold like stocks, providing investors with more flexibility.

Some risks of investing in ETFs include:

- Trading costs: Buying and selling ETFs can come with trading costs, such as commissions.
- Market volatility: Like stocks, the value of an ETF can fluctuate based on market conditions.

5. Real Estate

Real estate investments can include rental properties, commercial properties, and real estate investment trusts (REITs). Real estate can provide both rental income and potential capital appreciation.

Some benefits of investing in real estate include:

- Potential for rental income: Real estate investments can provide rental income, which can provide a steady stream of cash flow.
- Potential for capital appreciation: Real estate investments can also appreciate in value over time.
- Diversification: Real estate can provide diversification benefits to an investment portfolio.

Some risks of investing in real estate include:

- Maintenance costs: Real estate investments can come with maintenance costs and other expenses.
- Market volatility: The value of a real estate investment can

fluctuate based on market conditions.
- Lack of liquidity: Real estate investments can be illiquid, making it difficult to sell quickly.

6. Alternative Investments

Alternative investments can include hedge funds, private equity, and commodities. These investments can provide diversification benefits and the potential for high returns, but they also come with higher risks and fees.

Some benefits of investing in alternative investments include:

- Diversification: Alternative investments can provide diversification benefits to an investment portfolio.

- Potential for high returns: Some alternative investments, such as hedge funds and private equity, can provide the potential for high returns.

Some risks of investing in alternative investments include:

- Higher fees: Alternative investments can come with higher fees compared to traditional investments.
- Lack of liquidity: Alternative investments can be illiquid, making it difficult to sell quickly.
- Higher risk: Alternative investments can be riskier compared to traditional investments.

Choosing the Right Investments

When it comes to choosing the right investments, it's important to consider your personal financial goals, risk tolerance, and investment timeframe. Here are some tips to keep in mind:

1. **Determine your investment goals:** Consider your financial goals, such as saving for retirement or a down payment on a house. This will help you determine the types of investments that are best suited for you.

2. **Consider your risk tolerance:** How much risk are you willing to take on? Investments with higher potential returns often come with higher risk.

3. **Choose a diversified portfolio:** Diversification can help reduce risk in your portfolio. Consider investing in a mix of stocks, bonds, and other assets.

4. **Understand the fees:** Be aware of the fees associated with different investments. Fees can eat into your returns over time.

5. **Review your portfolio regularly:** It's important to review your portfolio regularly and make adjustments as needed to ensure it aligns with your goals and risk tolerance.

Conclusion

Investing can be a powerful tool to help you achieve your financial goals. By understanding the different types of investments and choosing the ones that are best suited for you, you can build a diversified portfolio that helps you achieve long-term success. Remember, investing comes with risks, so it's important to do your research and seek the advice of a financial professional before making any investment decisions. As Warren Buffett once said, "**Risk comes from not knowing what you're doing.**"

CHAPTER

Building Passive Income Streams

Passive income refers to income that is earned without active involvement or effort on your part. Building passive income streams can be a powerful way to achieve financial independence and freedom. In this chapter, we will explore different ways to build passive income streams, including real estate investing, dividend investing, rental income, and online businesses.

1. Real Estate Investing

Real estate investing can provide both rental income and potential capital appreciation. In addition to traditional rental properties, there are several other ways to invest in real estate:

- **Real Estate Investment Trusts (REITs):** REITs are companies that own and operate income-producing real estate properties. Investing in REITs can provide exposure to real estate without the hassle of owning and managing physical properties.

- **Real Estate Crowdfunding:** Real estate crowdfunding platforms allow investors to pool their money together to invest in real estate projects. This can provide access to real estate investments with lower minimum investments compared to traditional real estate investing.

2. Dividend Investing

Dividend investing involves investing in companies that pay dividends, which are regular payments made to shareholders. Dividends can provide a steady stream of passive income and can be reinvested to help grow your investment portfolio over time.

Some key considerations when it comes to dividend investing include:

- **Dividend yield:** This is the percentage of the stock price that is paid out in dividends each year. Higher dividend yields can provide more passive income but may come with higher risk.
- **Dividend growth**: This is the rate at which a company increases its dividend payments over time. Companies with a history of

consistent dividend growth can provide long-term passive income.

- **Dividend sustainability**: It's important to consider whether a company can sustain its dividend payments over the long term. Companies with strong financials and a history of consistent earnings can be more likely to sustain their dividend payments.

3. Rental Income

Rental income can provide a steady stream of passive income, but it also comes with responsibilities such as property management, maintenance, and tenant screening. Some key considerations when it comes to rental income include:

- **Location**: Location is key when it comes to rental properties. Properties in desirable locations with high demand can provide higher rental income and potential capital appreciation.

- **Cash flow**: It's important to consider the cash flow of a rental property, including expenses such as mortgage payments, property taxes, and maintenance costs.

- **Tenant screening**: Proper tenant screening can help reduce the risk of non-payment or property damage. Consider factors such as credit scores, rental history, and employment history when screening tenants.

4. Online Businesses

Online businesses can provide a variety of passive income streams, including affiliate marketing, digital product sales, and advertising revenue. Some key considerations when it comes to building online businesses include:

- **Niche selection**: Choosing a profitable niche can help increase the potential for passive income. Consider factors such as competition, market demand, and profit margins when selecting a niche.

- Content creation: High-quality content can help attract traffic and potential customers to your online business. Consider creating valuable content such as blog posts, videos, or e-books.

- Marketing and promotion: Effective marketing and promotion can help drive traffic and sales to your online business. Consider strategies such as social media marketing, search engine optimization, and paid advertising.

Quotes to Motivate YOU:

"Passive income is the key to achieving financial freedom and retiring early." - **Robert Kiyosaki**

"Investing in assets that generate passive income is the only way to build wealth." - **Grant Cardone**

"Creating passive income streams is the ultimate goal of any investor." - **Tony Robbins**

Conclusion:

Building passive income streams can be a powerful way to achieve financial independence and freedom.

Another way to generate passive income is by investing in real estate. This can include owning rental properties or investing in real estate investment trusts (REITs). Rental properties can provide a consistent stream of income through monthly rent payments, and if the property appreciates in value, the owner can sell it for a profit. However, owning rental properties requires active management and can come with unexpected expenses, such as repairs and maintenance.

Investing in REITs is a more passive way to invest in real estate. REITs are companies that own or finance income-producing real estate, such as apartments, office buildings, and shopping centers. By investing in a REIT, individuals can earn a share of the income produced by the underlying real estate without having to manage the properties themselves.

Another way to generate passive income is by creating and selling digital products, such as e-books, online courses, and software. Once the product is created, it can continue to generate income with minimal effort from the creator. This can be a particularly lucrative option for those with expertise in a particular field, as they can leverage their knowledge to create valuable products for others.

Finally, individuals can also generate passive income by investing in dividend-paying stocks or mutual funds. When a company earns a profit, it can choose to reinvest the profits back into the business or distribute them to shareholders in the form of dividends. By investing in dividend-paying stocks or mutual funds, individuals can earn a steady stream of income without having to actively manage their investments.

To effectively build passive income streams, individuals should consider diversifying their investments and choosing sources of passive income that align with their interests and expertise.

As the saying goes, "Don't put all your eggs in one basket." By spreading their investments across different assets and income streams, individuals can reduce their overall risk and increase their chances of achieving long-term financial success.

In addition to diversification, it's important to approach passive income with a long-term mindset. Building passive income streams takes time and effort, and there may be setbacks along the way. However, by staying focused on their goals and consistently working towards building passive income, individuals can create a sustainable source of income that provides financial freedom and flexibility.

As Robert Kiyosaki, author of the best-selling book **"Rich Dad Poor Dad,"** says: **"The rich don't work for money. They work to acquire assets that generate passive income."** By building passive income streams, individuals can work towards achieving financial freedom and creating a life of abundance and fulfillment.

CHAPTER

Planning For Retirement

Retirement may seem far away for those in their twenties or thirties, but it is never too early to start planning for it. Retirement planning involves setting goals and creating a financial plan to achieve those goals. In this chapter, we will discuss the importance of retirement planning, the different types of retirement plans, and strategies for saving for retirement.

Why Retirement Planning is Important

Retirement planning is important for several reasons. First, it allows individuals to maintain their standard of living after they stop working. Without retirement savings, individuals may have to rely solely on Social Security, which may not provide enough income to cover their expenses.

Second, retirement planning allows individuals to take advantage of compounding interest. Compounding interest occurs when the interest earned on an investment is reinvested, allowing the investment to grow exponentially over time. The earlier individuals start saving for retirement, the more time their investments have to grow through compounding interest.

Types of Retirement Plans

There are several types of retirement plans available, including:

1. **401(k) Plans**: 401(k) plans are employer-sponsored retirement

plans that allow employees to contribute a portion of their salary to their retirement account. Employers may also contribute to the account through matching contributions.

2. **Individual Retirement Accounts (IRAs)**: IRAs are personal retirement accounts that individuals can open through a financial institution. Contributions to a traditional IRA may be tax-deductible, while contributions to a Roth IRA are made with after-tax dollars and are tax-free when withdrawn.

3. **Simplified Employee Pension (SEP) Plan**: A SEP plan is a retirement plan for self-employed individuals and small business owners. Employers can contribute

up to 25% of an employee's salary to their SEP plan.

4. **Defined Benefit Plans**: Defined benefit plans are employer-sponsored retirement plans that provide a guaranteed income stream in retirement. The benefit amount is typically based on the employee's salary and years of service.

Saving Strategies for Retirement

To effectively save for retirement, individuals should consider the following strategies:

1. **Start Early**: The earlier individuals start saving for retirement, the more time their investments have

to grow. Even small contributions made in their twenties or thirties can compound significantly over time.

2. **Maximize Contributions**: Individuals should aim to contribute the maximum amount allowed to their retirement accounts each year. For example, in 2022, the maximum contribution limit for a 401(k) plan is $20,500.

3. **Take Advantage of Employer Contributions**: If an employer offers matching contributions to a 401(k) plan, individuals should aim to contribute at least enough to receive the full employer match.

4. **Diversify Investments**: It is important to diversify retirement investments to reduce risk. A well-diversified portfolio may include a mix of stocks, bonds, and mutual funds.

5. **Consider a Roth IRA**: A Roth IRA may be a good option for those who expect to be in a higher tax bracket in retirement. Because contributions to a Roth IRA are made with after-tax dollars, withdrawals in retirement are tax-free.

6. **Plan for Inflation**: Inflation can erode the value of retirement savings over time. Individuals should consider investing in assets that have historically kept pace with inflation, such as stocks.

7. **Review and Adjust the Plan**: Retirement planning is not a one-time event. Individuals should review their retirement plans periodically and make adjustments as necessary.

Conclusion

Retirement planning may seem daunting, but with the right strategies and mindset, individuals can effectively save for retirement and achieve financial freedom in their golden years. As Benjamin Franklin once said, "If you fail to plan, you are planning to fail." By taking the time to plan for retirement and consistently working towards their goals, individuals can enjoy a comfortable and fulfilling retirement.

CHAPTER

Managing Risks

When it comes to managing your finances, risk management is an essential aspect. No matter how much you plan, unexpected events such as market downturns, illnesses, or natural disasters can significantly impact your finances. Hence, it is important to have a plan in place to manage these risks effectively. This chapter will provide a comprehensive guide on managing risk and ensuring your financial security.

1. Understanding the types of risk:

The first step to managing risk is to understand the different types of risk you might face. Here are the major types of risks you need to know about:

- **Market risk**: This risk is associated with investing in stocks, bonds, and other financial instruments. It refers to the possibility of losing money due to fluctuations in the financial markets.

- **Credit risk**: This type of risk arises when a borrower defaults on their debt payments, leading to a loss for the lender.

- **Inflation risk**: Inflation is the rate at which the cost-of-living increases over time. This type of risk refers to the possibility that inflation will erode the value of your investments and savings.

- **Interest rate risk**: Interest rate risk refers to the possibility of losing money due to changes in interest rates. For example, if you have a fixed-rate loan, you may end up paying more if interest rates rise.

- **Liquidity risk**: This risk arises when you need to sell an asset quickly but are unable to do so without incurring a loss.

2. **Diversify your portfolio:**

Diversification is an important strategy for managing risk. By investing in a variety of assets, you can reduce your exposure to any one asset class. Diversification can be achieved by investing in different sectors, industries, and asset classes, such as stocks, bonds, and real estate.

3. **Consider insurance:**

Insurance is an essential tool for managing risk. It can protect you against financial losses due to unexpected events such as illness, accidents, or natural disasters. Some of the common types of insurance you should consider include:

- **Health insurance**: This can cover medical expenses and ensure you do not incur significant financial losses due to unexpected medical emergencies.
- **Life insurance**: This can provide financial security for your loved ones in the event of your untimely death.
- **Property insurance**: This can protect your home and other personal property against damage due to natural disasters, theft, or other unexpected events.

- **Liability insurance**: This can provide financial protection in case you are sued for damages or injuries caused by your actions.

4. **Establish an emergency fund:**

An emergency fund is a crucial part of managing risk. It is a reserve of cash that you set aside to cover unexpected expenses such as medical emergencies, job loss, or unexpected home repairs. Experts recommend having an emergency fund that can cover at least three to six months of your living expenses.

5. **Avoid high-risk investments:**

While it may be tempting to invest in high-risk investments that promise high returns, it is important to be cautious. High-risk investments can lead to significant losses and erode your financial security. It is advisable to invest in a mix of low-risk and high-risk investments to balance your risk.

6. **Regularly review your finances:**

Finally, it is essential to regularly review your finances and update your risk management plan as needed. This can help you stay on top of any changes in your financial situation and adjust your investments and insurance coverage accordingly.

Quotes to Motivate YOU:

"Risk comes from not knowing what you're doing." - **Warren Buffett**

"The biggest risk is not taking any risk. In a world that's changing really quickly, the only strategy that is guaranteed to fail is not taking risks." - **Mark Zuckerberg**

"The only way to permanently change the temperature in the room is to reset the thermostat." – **Harv Eker**

Conclusion

Managing risk is an important part of achieving financial success. By taking steps to identify, assess, and manage risk, you can help protect your finances and increase the likelihood of achieving your financial goals. Whether you're investing in the stock market, buying a home, or starting a business, understanding and managing risk can help you make informed decisions and achieve long-term financial success.

CHAPTER

Balancing Money and Life

Achieving financial success is not just about accumulating wealth, but also about living a balanced and fulfilling life. Balancing money and life means finding a way to enjoy life while also managing your finances responsibly. This chapter will explore the importance of balancing money and life and provide practical tips for achieving this balance.

1. Define what balance means to you

The first step in achieving a balance between money and life is to define what balance means to you. This will vary from person to person, and it's important to find a balance that works for your unique situation. Some people may prioritize their careers and financial goals, while others may prioritize their personal relationships and experiences.

It's important to identify your values and goals in life and create a plan that aligns with them. This will help you stay focused on what's important to you and make decisions that support your overall vision for a balanced life.

2. **Create a budget**

Creating a budget is an important part of balancing money and life. A budget helps you understand your income and expenses, and can help you make informed decisions about your spending. It's important to create a budget that allows you to save for your financial goals while also allowing you to enjoy your life.

When creating a budget, be sure to include both fixed and variable expenses. Fixed expenses are expenses that remain the same each month, such as rent or mortgage payments, while variable expenses can change from month to month, such as groceries or entertainment.

3. **Prioritize experiences over possessions**

While it's important to have the basic necessities in life, such as a home and a car, it's also important to prioritize experiences over possessions. Studies have shown that experiences bring more happiness than material possessions in the long run. This means spending money on things like travel, concerts, or other experiences that bring you joy.

When deciding how to allocate your money, think about what experiences would bring you the most happiness and try to prioritize those over material possessions.

4. **Set realistic financial goals**

Setting realistic financial goals is important for balancing money and life. It's important to set goals that are achievable and aligned with your values and priorities. This could include saving for a down payment on a home, paying off debt, or saving for retirement.

When setting financial goals, be sure to make them specific, measurable, and time-bound. This will help you stay motivated and focused on achieving your goals

5. **Find ways to save money**

Finding ways to save money is an important part of balancing money and life. This can include things like shopping around for the best deals on necessities like groceries or insurance or finding ways to cut back on discretionary spending.

One effective way to save money is to automate your savings. This means setting up automatic transfers from your checking account to your savings account each month. This can help you save money without having to think about it.

6. **Make time for self-care**

Taking care of your physical and mental health is an important part of balancing money and life. This can include things like exercising regularly, getting enough sleep, and practicing stress-reducing activities like meditation or yoga.

Making time for self-care can help you feel more energized and focused, which can in turn help you make better financial decisions.

7. Don't compare yourself to others

Comparing yourself to others can be a major source of stress and anxiety. It's important to remember that everyone's financial situation is different, and what works for one person may not work for another.

Instead of comparing yourself to others, focus on your own values and goals, and make decisions that are aligned with them.

8. Use automation to manage your finances

Automation is a powerful tool for managing your finances. It can help you stay on top of your bills, save money, and invest for the future. Here are some ways you can use automation to your advantage:

- Set up automatic bill payments: This will ensure that you never miss a payment and will help you avoid late fees and penalties.
- Use budgeting apps: There are a variety of budgeting apps available that can help you track your spending, set goals, and monitor your progress.
- Automate your savings: Set up automatic transfers from your checking account to a savings account or investment account.

This will help you save money without even thinking about it.

- Use robo-advisors: Robo-advisors are online investment platforms that use algorithms to manage your portfolio. They can help you invest your money in a diversified portfolio of stocks and bonds.

By automating your finances, you can save time, reduce stress, and improve your financial situation.

9. Seek professional advice

While there are many things you can do on your own to improve your financial situation, sometimes it's helpful to seek professional advice. A financial advisor can help you create a personalized financial plan based on your goals, risk tolerance, and financial situation.

A financial advisor can also help you with:

- Retirement planning: A financial advisor can help you determine how much you need to save for retirement and develop a plan to achieve that goal.
- Tax planning: A financial advisor can help you minimize your tax liability and take advantage of tax-advantaged investment accounts.
- Investment management: A financial advisor can help you manage your investments and ensure that they are aligned with your goals and risk tolerance.

When choosing a financial advisor, look for someone who is a fiduciary. This means that they are legally obligated to act in your best interests.

10. Monitor your progress

Finally, it's important to monitor your progress on a regular basis. This will help you stay motivated and make adjustments as needed. Here are some things you can do to monitor your progress:

- Review your financial goals regularly: Check in on your financial goals every few months to see how you're progressing. If you're not on track, adjust your plan accordingly.
- Monitor your spending: Keep track of your spending and look for ways to cut back on unnecessary expenses.
- Check your credit score: Your credit score is an important indicator of your financial health. Check it regularly to make sure it's in good shape.

- Review your investments: Keep an eye on your investments and make adjustments as needed to ensure that they are aligned with your goals and risk tolerance.

By monitoring your progress regularly, you can stay on track and achieve your financial goals.

Conclusion

Achieving financial success is a long-term process that requires dedication, discipline, and hard work. By following the tips outlined in this book, you can take control of your finances, build a strong financial foundation, and achieve your financial goals.

Remember, financial success is not about getting rich quick or taking unnecessary risks. It's about making smart decisions, living within your means, and investing for the future. With patience and perseverance, you can achieve financial freedom and enjoy a secure and prosperous future.

As Warren Buffett once said, **"Someone's sitting in the shade today because someone planted a tree a long time ago."** Start planting your financial tree today, and you'll be sitting in the shade tomorrow.

CHAPTER

Staying Motivated and on Track

In the journey towards financial success, it can be challenging to stay motivated and on track. There will be moments of doubt, setbacks, and temptations that can derail even the most disciplined person. However, it is essential to stay focused and committed to your goals to achieve financial success. This chapter will discuss various strategies for staying motivated and on track to achieve your financial goals.

Reflect on Your Why

One of the best ways to stay motivated is to remind yourself why you started the journey towards financial success. Think about your goals, both short-term and long-term, and the reasons why they matter to you. Reflect on the life you want to create for yourself and your loved ones. Visualize the future you want to create and use that as motivation to stay focused.

"Remembering why you started can be the driving force to keep you going." - Sahil A Gosalia

Celebrate Small Wins

It is crucial to celebrate your successes, no matter how small they may seem. Celebrating your accomplishments can help you stay motivated and on track. Recognize and appreciate the progress you have made, and use it as inspiration to keep going.

"Success is not final, failure is not fatal: it is the courage to continue that count." - Winston Churchill

Surround Yourself with Positive Influences

Surround yourself with people who support your goals and inspire you to achieve them. Seek mentors, coaches, or like-minded individuals who can provide guidance and motivation when you need it. Avoid negative influences that may discourage or distract you from your goals.

"You are the average of the five people you spend the most time with." - Jim Rohn

Create Accountability

Accountability can be a powerful motivator. Find someone who can hold you accountable for your actions and progress toward your goals. This can be a friend, family member, or financial advisor. Share your goals with them and ask for their support and guidance in achieving them.

"Accountability breeds response-ability." - Stephen Covey

Focus on Progress, Not Perfection

Perfectionism can be a roadblock to success. Instead of striving for perfection, focus on progress. Every small step you take toward your goals is progress, and it should be celebrated. Learn from your mistakes and keep moving forward.

"Perfection is not attainable, but if we chase perfection, we can catch excellence." - Vince Lombardi

Take Breaks

It is essential to take breaks and recharge your batteries. Burnout can lead to a lack of motivation and a decline in productivity. Take time to rest, reflect, and recharge. Engage in activities that bring you joy and energize you.

"Almost everything will work if you unplug it for a few minutes...including you." - Anne Lamott

Stay Focused on Your Goals

It is easy to get distracted by short-term pleasures or setbacks. However, it is crucial to stay focused on your long-term goals. Use reminders, such as visual cues or affirmations, to stay focused and motivated. Stay committed to your plan and be disciplined in your approach.

"Discipline is the bridge between goals and accomplishment." - Jim Rohn

Seek Inspiration

Seek inspiration from successful people who have achieved financial success. Read books, listen to podcasts, or attend events where you can learn from successful entrepreneurs, investors, or financial experts. Their stories and advice can provide motivation and inspiration to keep going.

"The only way to do great work is to love what you do." - Steve Jobs

Review your progress regularly:

Once you have established your financial goals, it's important to review your progress regularly. This will help you stay on track and make adjustments if necessary. You should review your progress at least once a year and adjust your goals if necessary.

It's also important to track your spending and savings to ensure that you are sticking to your budget. There are many tools available to help you do this, including budgeting apps, spreadsheets, and financial management software.

Stay motivated and on track:

Achieving financial success is a long-term journey, and it's important to stay motivated and on track. Here are some tips to help you stay motivated:

- Set short-term goals: Setting short-term goals can help you stay motivated and focused. Celebrate your small wins along the way, and use them as motivation to keep going.
- Surround yourself with positive influences: Surround yourself with people who are supportive of your goals and who will encourage you to keep going.
- Learn from setbacks: Setbacks and failures are inevitable, but they can also be valuable learning experiences. Use them as opportunities to learn and grow.
- Visualize your success: Visualize what financial success looks like for you, and keep that image in your mind. Use it as motivation to

keep going, even when the journey gets tough.

- Take care of yourself: Taking care of yourself is important for overall well-being and can also help you stay motivated. Make time for self-care activities, such as exercise, meditation, and spending time with loved ones.

Conclusion

achieving financial success at a young age is possible with the right mindset, strategies, and tools. It requires discipline, hard work, and a willingness to learn and adapt. By following the tips and strategies outlined in this book, you can set yourself up for financial success and a bright future. Remember, it's never too early or too late to start taking control of your financial future.

Achieving financial success at a young age and retiring at 35 is an ambitious goal, but it's not impossible. The key is to establish clear financial goals, build a strong financial foundation, maximize your income, manage your expenses, invest for the future, build passive income streams, plan for retirement, manage risk, balance money and life, and stay motivated and on track.

Through this book, we have explored each of these topics in detail and provided practical tips, tools, and strategies to help you achieve financial success. It's important to remember that financial success is a long-term journey, and it requires discipline, hard work, and a willingness to learn and adapt.

By following the tips and strategies outlined in this book, you can set yourself up for financial success and a bright future. Whether you're just starting out or you're looking to take your finances to the next level, the key is to take action and start making positive changes today.

Remember, it's never too early or too late to start taking control of your financial future. With the right mindset, strategies, and tools, you can achieve your financial goals and enjoy the freedom and security that comes with financial success.

So, what are you waiting for? Start your journey to financial success today!

Notes

Notes

Notes

Essential Calculators and Basic Understanding

1. **Compound Interest Calculator**: This calculator helps you calculate how much your money will grow over time with compound interest. The formula for compound interest is: A = P(1 + r/n)^(nt), where A is the final amount, P is the principal amount, r is the annual interest rate, n is the number of times interest is compounded per year, and t is the number of years.

Example: If you invest $10,000 at an annual interest rate of 6% compounded monthly for 10 years, your final amount will be: A = 10,000(1 + 0.06/12)^(12*10) = $18,209.09.

2. **Debt Payoff Calculator**: This calculator helps you determine how long it will take to pay off your debt and how much interest you will pay. The formula for calculating the total interest paid is: Total Interest = Total Payments - Principal, where Total Payments is the sum of all payments made over the life of the loan.

Example: If you have a $10,000 credit card balance with an interest rate of 18% and you make monthly payments of $250, it will take you 5 years and 5 months to pay off the debt, and you will pay $8,532.51 in interest.

3. **Retirement Savings Calculator**: This calculator helps you determine how much you need to save each month to reach your retirement goals. The formula for

calculating future value of your retirement account is: $FV = PV(1+r)^n$, where FV is the future value, PV is the present value, r is the annual interest rate, and n is the number of years.

Example: If you want to retire in 25 years and need $1 million in your retirement account, and assuming an average annual return of 7%, you need to save $1,327.03 per month to reach your goal.

4. **Mortgage Calculator**: This calculator helps you estimate your monthly mortgage payments based on the loan amount, interest rate, and loan term. The formula for calculating monthly mortgage payments is: $M = P[r(1+r)^n/((1+r)^n-1)]$, where M is the monthly mortgage payment,

P is the loan amount, r is the monthly interest rate, and n is the number of payments.

Example: If you take out a $200,000 mortgage with a 30-year term and an interest rate of 3.5%, your monthly mortgage payment will be $898.09.

"These calculators can be used to help you plan and make informed financial decisions."

Make The Best Use of The Book

To make the best use of this book, it is recommended to follow the chapters in sequence, as each chapter builds on the previous one to help you achieve financial success.

Take notes as you read, and use the action steps and exercises provided throughout the book to implement the concepts and strategies discussed.

In addition, don't hesitate to revisit chapters or sections as needed, and feel free to customize the advice to your unique circumstances and goals.

Remember that achieving financial success requires discipline, commitment, and perseverance. This book is intended to be a guide and resource to support you on your journey, but ultimately, the results depend on your actions and choices.

So, commit to applying the principles and strategies outlined in this book consistently and persistently, and you will be well on your way to achieving financial success and living the life of your dreams.

About the Author

Sahil A Gosalia is a seasoned financial professional with a passion for personal finance, investing, and wealth creation. With over a decade of experience in the finance industry, Sahil has helped numerous individuals and families achieve their financial goals and build wealth.

Sahil's journey towards financial success began at a young age when he realized the importance of financial literacy and smart money management. He has spent years studying various investment strategies, financial planning techniques, and wealth-building principles, which has helped him achieve financial success at a relatively young age.

The Author is known for his practical approach to personal finance and investing, and his ability to simplify complex financial concepts for readers of all levels of financial literacy. He is passionate about empowering individuals to take control of their financial future and make informed decisions about their money. Through his writing, the author aims to share his knowledge, insights, and strategies with readers to help them achieve financial success and live a financially secure life.

Apart from his professional pursuits, Sahil is an avid traveler and enjoys exploring new places, cultures, and cuisines. He also has a keen interest in philanthropy and giving back to the community.

With his wealth of experience and expertise in the field of personal finance and investing, Sahil A Gosalia is a trusted voice in the financial world and a respected author. His practical insights and actionable advice in this book will guide readers on their journey towards financial success and early retirement.

Summary

"My Journey Towards Financial Success at 35" is a comprehensive guide to achieving financial success at a young age. The book covers a wide range of topics, including establishing financial goals, building a strong financial foundation, maximizing income, managing expenses, investing for the future, building passive income streams, planning for retirement, managing risk, balancing money and life, and staying motivated and on track.

Each chapter provides practical advice, action steps, and exercises to help readers implement the concepts and strategies discussed. The book emphasizes the importance of discipline, commitment, and perseverance in achieving financial success, and provides readers with the knowledge, inspiration, and motivation needed to take control of their financial future and live the life of their dreams.

Scan to check more of my work!

Scan to BUY Books,
E-Books, Journals,
Notebooks

Scan to know more about the Author

www.ingramcontent.com/pod-product-compliance
Lightning Source LLC
LaVergne TN
LVHW090410210926
848480LV00002B/523
* 9 7 9 8 2 2 3 6 6 7 9 9 5 *